The daughter

My mother was a fisherman

my father was the sea

Among the Dead:

Ah!
and Afterward
Yes!

Becca Jensen

Les Figues Press
Los Angeles

Winner of the 2011 NOS Les Figues Press Book Contest
as selected by Sarah Shun-lien Bynum.

NOS: Not Otherwise Specified.

Cover and Typesetting: Emma Williams

Among the Dead: Ah! and Afterward Yes!
FIRST EDITION

ISBN 13: 978-1-934254-38-7
ISBN 10: 1-934254-38-X
Library of Congress Control Number: 2012952075

Les Figues Press thanks its members for their support and readership.
Les Figues Press is a 501c3 organization. Donations are tax-deductible.

Les Figues would like to acknowledge the following individuals for their generosity: Peter Binkow
and Johanna Blakley, Lauren Bon, Chris and Diane Calkins, and Coco Owen.

Les Figues Press titles are available through:
Les Figues Press, <http://www.lesfigues.com>
Small Press Distribution, <http://www.spdbooks.org>

Special thanks to Harold Abramowitz, Alyssa Brillinger, Jennifer Calkins, Teresa Carmody, Gabrielle
Glickstein, Veronica Gonzalez, Elizabeth Hall, Militza Jean-Felix, Erin Kilduff, Vanessa Place, Janet
Sarbanes, and Emma Williams.

Post Office Box 7736
Los Angeles, CA 90007
info@lesfigues.com
www.lesfigues.com

To my own parental figures, M & P.

And to Ryan.

CONTENTS

FOREWORD

BY SARAH SHUN-LIEN BYNUM

Becca Jensen describes this book as taking place inside a family of five: Mrs. G, Mr. G, the daughter, the Collector, and the Chorus. The word "family" is a wonderful way to suggest the relationship among the multiple entities that we encounter within: family as both structure and story. In one of the book's first pieces, "How To Persuade an Abstraction," the Chorus instructs us to take abstraction by the throat, to take hold of "tales and other ends" as it slithers past us. For it is through story that we wrestle best with abstraction, and the powerful family narrative that Jensen builds here is her means of considering loneliness and lack, the impossible search for beginnings, exile and foreignness, and the ecstatic apprehension of a world in which everything (as the Collector paraphrases Proust) "seems to be folded into everything."

This narrative is built, with the assiduous help of the Collector, out of fragments and allusions drawn largely from the Western canon: the Bible, the *Odyssey*, Spenser and Shakespeare and Milton, the English Romantic poets, Melville, the Modernists. The literary fragment is itself a sort of exile, existing as it does outside of its original source, denatured by quotation marks, or made noticeable by a difference in rhythm and syntax, or foreign-seeming simply by virtue of its familiarity: the reader's vague but strong sense of *don't I know you from someplace else?*

The Collector heightens this sense of the familiar (and the familial) through his unusual method for cataloging the source materials. Though he is careful in documenting the origins of each fragment, his catalogs do not directly or obviously correspond to the order in which the fragments appear throughout the book; often we are introduced to the source long before we come across the fragment, or else we are surprised to learn that an image we liked twenty-five pages earlier in fact hails from Milton's *Lycidas*. The Collector offers us not an index of allusions but rather an atmosphere. We are immersed in it, surrounded by it; the Collector's lists flow in and out of the narrative, both beginning and ending the book, enveloping it. This atmosphere of allusion produces the feeling of reading great books: of being inside an enormous bell, a bell cast from the world's wide store of epics and elegies and tales and novels, unable to tell where one's own voice ends and the reverberations begin.

The fragment is an exile but it is also a consolation. It reminds us of the family that, through the act of reading, we come home to. Yes, this book is haunted by loss, by orphans and shipwrecks and drowning, yet when one's "mother is a fisherman" and one's "father is the sea," drowning can be a kind of homecoming.

Among the Dead:

                              Ah!
                              and Afterward
                                       Yes!

THE COLLECTOR: WHEREFROM

"after three hours she curtsied profoundly and left." Virginia Woolf, *Orlando*

"'ah! and afterward yes!'": "The gentleman put up his eye-glasses to look at me, and said, 'Come here, my dear!' He shook hands with me, and asked me to take off my bonnet—looking at me all the while. When I had complied, he said, 'Ah!' and afterwards 'Yes!'" from Charles Dickens' *Bleak House*

Ahab, captain of *The Pequod* in Herman Melville's *Moby Dick*. Ahab, along with his crew, drowns when *The Pequod* sinks from damages incurred from the leviathan Moby Dick. Only Ishmael, the main character and semi-narrator of *Moby Dick*, survives. The last word of Melville's novel: orphan

all of Odysseus' men: after sacrificing six men to the six-headed monster, Scylla, Odysseus and his crew arrive on the island Thrinakia, where the god Helios (a.k.a Hyperion) keeps his sacred cattle. Though he warns them not to, Odysseus' men eat the cattle. Back at sea, Zeus punishes the offenders by sinking the ship and drowning all the men but Odysseus. Odysseus' narration of his past exploits ends with this story; the rest of *The Odyssey* pertains to Odysseus' present course of action in Ithaca

"all the rest is commentary" is from Hillel, a Jewish religious teacher of the 1st century B.C.E. When asked to summarize the Torah, Hillel replies: "What is hateful to you, do not do to your neighbor. This is the whole Torah; all the rest is commentary"

"among the Dead" comes from T.S. Eliot's "Tradition and the Individual Talent," from *The Sacred Wood: Essays on Poetry and Criticism* (1920): "No poet, no artist of any art, has his complete meaning alone. His significance, his appreciation is the appreciation of his relation to the dead poets and artists. You cannot value him alone; you must set him, for contrast and comparison, among the dead"

"and in my breast / Spring…" is from No. 115 of *In Memoriam A. H. H.*, Tennyson. The line ends with the word "rest"

"angel of its face" refers to Isaiah 63:9, also commonly translated as "the angel of his presence"

THE CHORUS: HOW TO PERSUADE AN ABSTRACTION

"You take it by the throat," says I! "The throat
by which it lies." You find that slithering moon, find that tearing
sky and "gosh, gosh, gosh, gosh—"

"Hold it," I say, still! "Tight by the belly" until it opens
like the sky. Then dear expedience curl it "past yourself, past"
your resting roundness, and let it come, roundly roundly:

But remember peace good gosh, peace
good you. For in the slithering sky does lie that "easy, open
moon," just waiting to be missed

"So says I, says still:" take hold
of tales and other ends; for that, dear princess—is the world gone round, "round
like the moon when it tears" itself out of the sky

MRS. G AS YOUNG GLYNIS YOUNG

I. Fragments

> Once, and but once
> upon a time, a heart upon,
> upon a head. Came hand
> in truth,
> amen.

"How like a shepherd am I," claims Glynis Young, "how
innocent I bend. Look!
how I allow nature to outdo herself."

> the high lawns, the early
> cherry, and then the later plum,
> but always still and always always
> and amen

---

the hills rolling into parcels
of pure sky

MR. G: OPTION A OR THERE IS SOMETHING IN GOD THAT IS NOT GOD

James places the last purple shadow on the violet's outer wing. He has spent some time thinking about the round corners of its soft shell, the forest floor held in a pool of its waxy leaves where later he would go and search for mushrooms, feeling the damp earth, the hint of sunlight, moving like desire around his kneecaps or what Hegel calls the twofold significance of the distinct. How

    1. we remain ourselves only in contrast

        -thereby-

    2. becoming contrast ourselves.

James watches what he is not move beneath the violet's tender neck, radiant between the landscapes of the park and the outer mountains. It constitutes itself as an interior, which is the rotting wood of the picnic bench, the sky among its blue globules. Meanwhile:

    some wind throws a juniper into itself.

Meanwhile the violet dries into the thin white bone of the teacup, its rim looking like a shaved tooth. Nearby, a few seabirds push their dense feathers between the pillow of James' skin

    a.   like long and gray
    b.   among the sun
    c.   feeding in flight.

Pale clouds churn through the wandering air and there is a feeling with James that is like the difference between emptiness and space or what one looks like with the other inside it— "Hello," he says to the crowd through which the familiar beckons: the dulled afternoon light falling from his face.

JAMES' FACE

abcdefghijklmnopqrstu
vwxyzzyxwvutsrqpo
nmlkjihgfedcba*******
****
****
****
****
******
**

The angel of its face. The grind of the prison house. Yes, first the eyes must go. Fetters and brass. The body—soft plume of a high tower and cut down the center toward the faint

round of its belly. Read: again, on top of. Rib of rock. Then the red sails. Rusty treasure. A certain shade of grief. And afterwards: a creature stirring up. Its thick thighs and open toes.

Dusty at the fingertips. And afterwards: what to do with an analyzed soul? On the way hence. Read: on top of. Yes, to set with dogs. To tear into its crown. This is the general

sense, but not the exact order of, a lonely war.

II. All the Rest is Commentary

Hills mean slants and slant means: (n) a person who is comfortable amidst the gravitational pull
of meaning. So, OK, Glynis Young is a mound-o-meaning, thus she innocently bends. But that
was once but once, so what is now still now? Perhaps the sky? Sky being the infinite bound by
limitations, i.e. My dear, my darling, spend your limited eternity with me. But this turn into sky
happens "always still and always always," a quadruple positive, which equals a negative. Therefore
mathematically speaking, we are in the past. And if we only can locate Glynis in the past, can
she exist? Yes, we have her direct quote, but because of her penchant for similes she leaves us on
shadowed ground. The only thing we really know about her is what she claims she is not: nature.
If we take her at her word, then she could be art. But the idea that art is inferior to nature is no
longer of the fashionable intelligence, and consequently must be ignored. Of course we also find
Glynis among the listed fruit—that obvious nod toward Eve—but that is an archetype, and one
should avoid archetypes when dealing with Mrs. G.

Her finely tipped points. The way her heart cut up the sky—in fixed bloom. Lay her

in lilies and in violets and in praise—the trees so straight and tall, her modest eyes.

Yes, on either side the river lie: 1. So, over that art which you say adds to nature, is an

art that nature makes. 2. Which be the flowers, as it were, and colors that a poet

setteth upon his language by art. It is difficult, but above all, one must remember that

behind those lawyerly arguments, those thrashing sides, sits bold in her own daylight:

a woman. She adjusts her skirts. Like a god the beauty of the world—out of the earth

a fabric huge. Lace upon lace. Suppose in silks or tissues and costly embroideries.

Arid, rocky. A slight pink at times and on a sudden red. Or green thick in tangles

green. Her head a kind of stern wilderness. One is constrained to praise. Like a god,

beauty. Some tone on a hill. Canyons. Bleak-grown pines. The sea salt blue. All that

wide and golden scales. All that resolving down into herself. Location being the

problem. On either side the river lie: 3. The endless tyranny of a landscape. 4. Long

fields of barley and of rye that clothe the wold and meet the sky and through the field

the road runs by

MR. GRUMBLE GRUMBLES

Like many heroes who find themselves haphazardly at the center of a plot,
Mr. G concluded that

        a) this was a very stupid story

                        &

        b) he didn't care to hear it again.

THE CHORUS: REVISIT THUS THE GLIMPSES OF THE MOON

We learn that James takes a walk during which he is transformed by the beauty of a violet. The experience transports himself outside himself—what most associate with the experience called love, but what the Greeks more accurately understood as ecstasy. Though it should be noted that accuracy is a misnomer in such cases. Here is the Greek translation:

> Dawn.

> James as walking.

> A violet and he sees himself as if words on a page.

> Night pursues in thickets of interpretation.

> Dawn explains herself.

> The violet as an idea makes a case for creating Mr. G.

> A complaint is heard about over complication.

The pattern that moves around the above should be understood as Either/Or, e.g. either there is dawn or dawn explaining.

Meanwhile, though at least sixteen years later, the daughter will try to make sense of it all by pretending she is a sailor. Occasionally she goes on land and buys a banana, though mostly, she talks to her shadow, the collector. She even interviews him for her radio show. He is very insightful, callers say. See for yourself:

and in my breast / Spring wakens too; and my regret / Becomes an April violet, / And buds
and blossoms like the

THE COLLECTOR: I

"arriving at each new city, the traveler finds again a past of his that he did not know he had: the foreignness of what you no longer are or no longer possess": Italo Calvino, *Invisible Cities*

Bertha Mason grows up in Jamaica and marries Edward Rochester, only to find herself insane and locked in the attic of Thornfield Hall, her husband's estate in England, which she eventually burns down along with herself. She is one of several symbols that Charlotte Brontë uses in *Jane Eyre* to demonstrate the inferiority of foreign, non-British peoples. Almost a hundred years later, Bertha makes a more sympathetic appearance in Jean Rhys' *Wide Sargasso Sea*

"…bleak-grown pines" is taken from John Keats' *Hyperion: Book II*. Saturn has just announced to his fallen colleagues: "Titans, behold your God!" to which Keats writes:

> There is a roaring in the bleak-grown pines
> When Winter lifts his voice; there is a noise
> Among immortals when a God gives sign,
> With hushing finger, how he means to load
> His tongue with the full weight of utterless thought,
> With thunder, and with music, and with pomp:
> Such noise is like the roar of bleak-grown pines
> Which, when it ceases in this mountain'd world,
> No other sound succeeds (ln 116-124)

"…choosing a firm cloud (before it falls!)": the "moral essays" of Alexander Pope's *Epistle II: To a Lady* (ln 19)

Dante Alighieri, Italian poet of the 13th/14th centuries, is condemned to perpetual exile from his home in Florence for politically positioning himself against the Black Guelphs, the Florentine faction in support of the Papacy, and therefore Rome. He escapes from his life as an exile by writing *The Divine Comedy*, which, among other things, performs various acts of vengeance on his persecutors. Years later, he dies, still in exile

Don Juan is a fictional Spanish libertine. In Byron's version he is not a womanizer but a compliant object of women's desires, or more to the point, a tool for "satire on abuses of the present state of Society." Byron's Don Juan appears in almost two thousand stanzas and could have had more if Byron had not died in 1824, having lived the last eight years of his life in a self-inflicted state of exile

THE DAUGHTER

There are things that follow me: five
pelicans on top a flat roof, one shoving its opened mouth back

down its neck. There are things that follow
me—I am not one of them. I have held 161

whole shells, including two
store-bought cartons filled with perfectly shaped bodies: pearled

then fluorescent then the edge striped
with coral. The collector wears a broad shadow; it comes

from his hat, though he has small
curved hands that have something to do with water. They follow

the lines of my collarbone, smooth out
my pillow. We cross the street. We buy a banana

for 59 cents. Meaning
finds us despite itself—swollen

in its daily pursuits, becoming
delicate, gummy with time: our little rat breath.

THE COLLECTOR: TAKE

"each day she works a heart between her teeth" is from the following poem by Charles Baudelaire, translated by James McGowan. Richard Howard's interpretation, "[You'd sleep with anyone at all, you slut!]," is also worth reading

> You'd entertain the universe in bed,
> Foul woman; ennui makes you mean of soul.
> To exercise your jaws at this strange sport
> Each day you work a heart between your teeth.
> Your eyes, illuminated like boutiques
> Or blazing in a public fair,
> Use haughtily a power not their own,
> With no awareness of their beauty's law.
> …
> When Nature, mighty in her secret plans,
> Makes use of you, o woman! queen of sins!
> - Of you, vile beast - to mould a genius?
>
> O filthy grandeur! o sublime disgrace

"early cherry, and then the later plum" is from Ben Jonson's *To Penshurst* (ln 41)

Egyptian army (and Pharaoh?): In their pursuit of the Israelites across the Red Sea, the pursuing Egyptian army drowns. Scholars disagree as to whether or not the Pharaoh would have joined his troops in battle and therefore also would have died

"even though he has long had to stir with his arms the frost-cold sea, to tread the tracks of exile, fully-fixed is his fate" is from the Old English poem *The Wanderer*, one of the most harrowing illustrations of the utter loneliness the exile faces

"everything, except Noah et al" refers to the flood in Genesis, chapters 6-9. Unlike Abraham who, upon hearing God's plan to destroy the towns of Sodom and Gomorrah, asks something along the lines of, "would you destroy the righteous with the wicked," Noah never questions God's plan to exterminate almost all of creation

MRS. G: THEN, OPTION B OR THE LOSS OF A LOSS

All was. Was, amen. All was cedar wood
and china. The soundless blue of a white cloud
as it's thrown into relief. So she keeps herself unto
herself, at breakfast and always. Until one day

loneliness—her golden hand—reaches warm
to the ground. Quietly, his slim body wrapped
in her morning skirt wide with dew.

                    (She had only to want *something*—
                        in the beginning it mattered not what.)

But without loneliness she was unto herself
no longer. A hot pursuit of a hand—this version
of her former self: his greased eyebrows, his sunburned
throat. She leans: a fresh sincerity over a field

while the air mingles with mud-worn shoes.

HALLELU, HALLELU, HALLELUJAH:
THE CHORUS SINGS FOR MR. G IN SIGNS OF SIX

So God created man in his own image, in the image of God he created him; male
and female he created them. And there was evening and there was morning, a sixth day.

Our story—ours because of what we know—begins
with madness. With a mad king in a round
tower, who runs the halls with loss,
who some call God—
his crooked spine, his slant
walk that turns the sky wide

blue. Of course, this story bends far and wide
with lies. A lie to begin
in madness, to say this world slants
past sense. It does not! does not round
the truth and end in God.
And there is no such thing as loss!

Or rather everything in all is loss
so forgetting is no ruin, so loss and truth are wide
and run with God, behind the face of God!
until eventually, somehow, this face or loss or sky becomes our beginning—
a story crowned
with time gone slant.

So it is the event that is the lie, the thing aslant
while the tower goes about the king as if he were lost
as if the air was roundly
wide;
as if the truth began
as a madness we could not remember called God.

For there is always a before, so God
is the name for what slants
into a past—for a way of beginning—
with forgetting
as the spine that turns the pages wide
into a world rounded

into sense; and so we go in rounds, in rounds
of God is past, our Past is god—
and all can say the lie is wide
or all can say the truth is slant.
For ours is a madness that leaves out lack
and so our story ends as it begins.

Begin!—Round—from loss! round like exiles—
we don't need God, his widely truthful slants—we!
can destroy ourselves.

THE DAUGHTER AND HER JOURNEY FROM ALL THREE SIDES

I. The Water Keeps Narcissus with Its Empty Face

    1. Larboard and starboard all set to the sky

    2. Spritsail foresail through—full—and by

    3. Prosperous gales and a fly follow quick

    4. Ballast broad off and the hull spreading thick

    5. Bulkheads and midship searching an end

    6. Jib & boom & stern we depend

    7. Hammocks! nettings! a-bubble! squeak!

    8. Land's back dwindled, bleak

II. What Exile from Himself Can Flee?

1. …even though he has long had to stir with his arms the frost-cold sea, to tread the tracks of exile, fully-fixed is his fate…

2. Bertha Mason

3. Dante Alighieri

4. Walter Benjamin

5. Frankenstein

6. Okonkwo

7. Arriving at each new city, the traveler finds again a past of his that he did not know he had: the foreignness of what you no longer are or no longer possess…

8. Hester Prynne

9. Isaiah

10. Don Juan (Byron's)

Q: What's your favorite thing in your collection? A: You. Q: OK, fine. What's your second

favorite? A: That changes. Today I've been thinking about a clear plastic plant stand that is

covered in rows of cacti. It sits in front of a large window overlooking a yard that is cut off

fairly quickly by a line of mangy looking evergreen trees. It is the kind of place that you can't

imagine children playing in. Q: Is that what it always looked like? A: No, that's what it

looked like after I collected it. Before it was a thin mist over a cliff in Switzerland. Q: Is that

what Alexander Pope meant by his directive to choose a firm cloud before it falls? A: It's

what it means to look something in the eyes and know it doesn't exist.

(radio silence)
(radio silence)
(radio silence)
(radio silence)
(radio silence)
(radio silence)
(radio silence)
(radio silence)

(Stage directions: Cue the slow romp of salt water making its way against
the boat's frame. Stage left: the collector. Now come the field mice to
nibble at the puddles forming around his feet. When taken as a whole, fame
always seems slight. Or woven with veins. The violet and pink transparency
of mice ears trimming his ankles like a flourishing sock. Elsewhere, hills
and tufts of grass or a potted vine hang against a windowpane.)

"forest hung upon his head" is from John Keats' unfinished epic *Hyperion* (ln 6). Prior to the story's opening, the Olympians overthrew the Titans. Most of Keats' epic depicts the Titans' despair over this recent loss of power. This line refers to Saturn, the Titans' ruler

Frankenstein or fiend, as he more commonly is referred to in Mary Shelley's novel of that same name, is bound to a kind of unending exile by his sheer repulsiveness. As the subtitle of the novel indicates, our monster-hero is caught up in a retelling of Prometheus, and as such, is supposed to serve as a note of warning to humanity for its insatiable curiosity. But Frankenstein's ugliness also links him to another narrative—which perhaps climaxed with Grendel—that describes in gory detail the horrors of the outcast

"gosh, gosh, gosh, gosh" is from Marcel Proust's *Swann's Way* (1913), volume I of *In Search of Lost Time*. The narrator, Marcel, utters the words on one of his autumn walks, which are "all the more delightful because I used to take them after long hours spent over a book." This particular exclamation overwhelms Marcel when he comes across a sublime post-rain scene in which everything—the tool hut's tin roof, the pond, the sun, the sky—seems to be folded into everything. "Gosh, gosh, gosh, gosh!" says the overwhelmed narrator, who then thuds into the disquieting realization that there is often "a discordance between our impressions and their habitual expression"

"…grind of the prison house. Yes, first the eyes must go. Fetters and / brass" is taken from the story of Samson, Judges 16:21

Hamnet: William Shakespeare's only son born in 1585 along with his twin sister Judith. Hamnet dies at age 11 from the bubonic plague in 1596. Much has been made of the connection between Hamlet and Hamnet, most famously—at least in terms of literature—by Stephen Dedalus in James Joyce's *Ulysses*

"heart upon, / upon a head" is a derivative from Shakespeare's song in *The Merchant of Venice*: "Tell me where is fancy bred, / Or in the heart or in the head?"

Hester Prynne means A is for adulteress in Nathaniel Hawthorne's *The Scarlet Letter*

III. So the Moon of Her Exile Met the Sky with Light

So she sung:

> *The moon is an exile*
> > *but a well in the desert nonetheless.*

So there were sails and a moon and a song.

So her ship moved with a magnificent underbelly through the desert of her song:

> *The moon is a moon*
> > *until it is not. Then*

it is a hole

a nunnery to the truth for a bit
        of daydreaming and hence.

The Collector: Lore

"high lawns" comes from *Lycidas* by John Milton (ln 25)

"how dull it is to pause, to make an end," Alfred Lord Tennyson, *Ulysses* (ln 22)

Isaiah is given to us in one, two or three parts—depending on your interpretation. During his middle incarnation, Isaiah offers words of comfort to those living in exile in Babylon

"I've Done Nothing But Contradict Reality from the Outset" comes from José Saramago, *Death with Interruptions*, in which death stops working within the borders of an unnamed country. The Catholic Church refutes the news for theological reasons—if there is no death, there can be no resurrection. When asked by the Prime Minister how he plans to continue to operate, the cardinal replies: "We've done nothing but contradict reality from the outset"

"…jingling sound of like endings," says John Milton in his 1764 second edition preface to *Paradise Lost* ("The Verse"). Here Milton justifies the ways of blank verse to men as opposed to rhyme, or "Rime," which he calls "the Invention of a barbarous Age"

"kings shouldered out" comes from *Beowulf* (translated by Seamus Heaney):

> Shield was still thriving when his time came
> and he crossed over into the Lord's keeping.
> His warrior band did what he bade them
> when he laid down the law among the Danes:
> they shouldered him out to the sea's flood,
> the chief they revered who had long ruled them (ln 26-31)

"like a god the beauty of the world" William Shakespeare, *Hamlet* (II, ii)

"lonely and en route" is from Paul Celan, translated by Rosmarie Waldrop: "The poem is lonely. It is lonely and en route. Its author stays with it" (Das Gedicht ist einsam. Es ist einsam und unterwegs. Wer es schreibt, bleibt ihm mitgegeben)

"long live the weeds and the wilderness yet" Gerard Manley Hopkins, "Inversnaid"

Lycidas, an elegiac poem by John Milton (1638) dedicated to Edward King, Milton's friend from college, who drowns in a shipwreck off the Welsh coast

In the study I found a
large picture of their
parents, with sexes
reversed, Mrs. G
resembling Malenkov,
and Mr. G a medusa-
locked hag, and this
I replaced by the
reproduction of a
beloved early Picasso:
earth boy leading
raincloud horse.
Nabokov, *Pale Fire*

The Chorus: Possess It Merely

The possible yellow house
I could sing there once was and how
I've forgotten to mention for a long time a thread
into the sun a hill a sleekest and best
little day-boat but most overwhelming of all
how I made it _ _ _ / _ _ toe-top Dear Madame the incidental interest
and history and chance may have it the air
tastes good consolation dear
in the usual terms but the beginning
I say of which there is none no golden rocks
quite generally supposed no to rest your head upon
only possibility a fancifulness of fangs and flaggy dragons flaggy dragons
and sticky pawed caves and look at me look at me
I hold it by its soft, damp temples.

	Statements/Daughter		Reasons/Shadow
1.	The lampshade is now unavailable to the mouse. It belongs to the nightstand just as the wall belongs to the light that crosses the lampshade.	1.	Our pattern is place and place is circumscription: the cool moss shuffles beneath the frog's webbed feet.
2.	Above the docks are windows where women sit. There are days in which the only thing that matters is their thin blue frames, the air thick with the arrival of rotting flesh.	2.	Origin: what x has lost on its way to becoming y :: we know where we are by the things that surround us, the moldering pool of purple thickets.
3.	The collector has a mustache that looks like the wily, abandoned legs of a deer tick.	3.	A stone is a moment in time as we approach it, reflecting first some dried grass then a man's hat as its roughed feather shakes the wind around it.
4.	… as they prepare the dead king to be shouldered out, a dash of rubies thrown into the eye sockets…	4.	Given
5.	At a certain point, yet to be determined, the curve where the city meets the sky seems to matter as a sign of something else.	5.	The story is the trace of x back to y until it becomes z, losing in the process both x and y. The story is a gesture of an object as it moves under a sea of turtles.

The Collector: And

Maggie Tulliver is the main character in Eliot's *The Mill on the Floss*. When the river Floss floods, Maggie attempts to save her estranged brother Tom, whose home lies dangerously near the flood's course of destruction. (Despite the fact that Tom has recently disowned Maggie for what he deemed sexually loose behavior.) Once she rescues him, the water capsizes their boat and they drown. Their bodies are "found in close embrace" and buried in a tomb inscribed with: "In death they were not divided." Because Tom has a history of withholding affection and approval from Maggie, and since the exact particulars of their deaths are unclear, it could be interpreted that the dead siblings' "close embrace" is not mutual. That after the boat overturned, only Maggie clung to Tom, while in all likelihood he tried to free himself from her grasp. With this reading in mind, the flood does not kill Tom Tulliver, Maggie does

"much turning of the head from side to side": George Eliot, *The Mill on the Floss*

"nightfall" comes from Allen Mandelbaum's verse translation of *The Odyssey*. Before each book begins, the subsequent action is summarized and listed in a kind of table of contents. Nightfall is the last event listed in Book VII

"night so long our roome did fill": Edmund Spenser's *The Faerie Queene*, Book I, Canto II

Okonkwo is from a fictional village in Nigeria and is the main character in Chinua Achebe's *Things Fall Apart*. He and his family are sent into exile after Okonkwo accidentally kills someone. When he returns seven years later, he finds his homeland irrevocably changed due to the influence of colonial powers, so, in a sense, he never returns home

"once, and but once" is from the opening line of John Donne's *Elegy IV: The Perfume*

"one-breasted Amazon": according to myth, Amazons burn or cut off the right breast to improve their archery skills

"one is constrained to praise" is a revision on Ralph Waldo Emerson's 1838 "Divinity School Address": "One is constrained to respect the perfection of this world"

"on either side the river lie / Long fields of barley and of rye, / that clothe the wold and meet the sky; / and through the field the road runs by" are the opening lines of Lord Alfred Tennyson's *The Lady of Shalott*

Mr. G: The Bottomless Gulf of His Paunch

I come out of the blue and see I am a whale. A whale in waves

of blue madonnas without a nose with jaws the royal blue

of ocean waves. I am full of blubber and bibles and Jonah

solemn as night reads both to me. We hear the continents

fall apart—they don't know how to groan enough. I am a whale

and Jonah has lowly bent eyes. He asks such questions, such:

"How do you build an island from scratch?" I am strained by his beauty

by his wrapped in seaweed body. And it seems I have a childish belief

in the way he sits upon my tongue: *weak life that leans*

on uncertain things—surrounded in raw gobbets and flesh. I touch your ears—

Mine, mine, mine.

Young Glynis Young: Her Favorite Story

So in this version the one-breasted Amazon speaks only
to the moon. She says,

I touch the stars
and dream of you.

But the moon does not care to respond. The moon, moon
is a great fanged wolf moon, cold and faceless with sets of fur upon
its tongue.

Eats stones for dinner.

"Again," says the daughter. They are lying in bed. Glynis points to a star
on the comforter: "See this star? This is the one-breasted
Amazon. Each day she works a heart

between her teeth."

The end is always the same—dragging home with cracked shoes; bloated, salty lips;
and three fresh bruises
on her right, inner arm. Home. Even now she hovers round

the taste of limes
and fish and tales of giants that burn her tongue. How she came to them
in a silver boat with scales of rainbow

about its sides. How they met her with a grace that is their proportion
but she ran for fear and hid
for fear beneath a fallen leaf, and when they found her, she spat in their faces and bit

their fingernails to the quick.
Yet they loved her anyway because she was small and precious and they called
her orphan, built

her a house out of chartreuse and sand. Then one of them—the one

no one liked—ate

her boat. After, how they came each hour with bodies heavy with worry, and what

could they do?

So she asked about her parents and where she could find them

until the giants collected

some stories. Her mother was the past and wore hair the color of mountaintops
and skin that ran like sunlight. Her father
was God and was made up of loss, which made him somewhat

forgetful, but mostly
he was kind. Then they built her another boat and kissed her in three places
on her right, inner arm.

"O O O O O O O O" awkwardly follows Hamlet's "—the rest is silence" in Shakespeare's 1623 First Folio. The line is often extracted from modern editions based on the assumption that someone else—an actor, stage manager—inserted those idiotic O's. Another reading gives them not to the younger, but to the elder Hamlet, whom the play leaves howling over his dead son's body

"o so wonderfully tired was he," Robert Walser, *Speaking to the Rose*

"…out of the earth a fabric huge" is from John Milton, *Paradise Lost*: Book I. After much stage setting, in this line, Hell's castle meets the air:

> Anon out of the earth a fabric huge
> Rose like an exhalation, with the sound
> Of dulcet symphonies and voices sweet—
> Built like a temple, where pilasters round
> Were set, and Doric pillars overlaid
> With golden architrave; nor did there want
> Cornice or frieze, with bossy sculptures graven;
> The roof was fretted gold (ln 710-17)

Paul Celan, aka Paul Antschel, poet, 1920-1970. Romanian born and Jewish, Celan survives his life in a WWII labor camp (though his immediate family does not). He commits suicide by drowning in the river Seine

Percy Bysshe Shelley, poet, 1792-1822. His boat, *Don Juan*, sinks due to a combination of storm and bad seamanship, and as a result Shelley and his two friends drown off the coast of Italy

"…praise—the trees so straight and tall" begins a longer tribute to the trees of Edmund Spenser's *The Faerie Queene*: Book I, Canto I

> Much can they praise the trees so straight and hy,
> The sayling pine, the cedar proud and tall,
> The vine-propp elme, the poplar never dry,
> The builder oake, sole king of forrests all,
> The aspine good for staves, the cypresse funerall (ln 104-8)

Mrs. G: In Greek Mythology

This time the river is her mouth. Cigarettes mostly. And a coral-red lipstick
wandering past her lips. Every year on her birthday
she swallows a brand new Pink Pearl eraser. All those unused bodies stacked against
her stomach wall. She is too old to be playing such tricks
but nevertheless by now she has learned a few things. When she does speak
the ferryman carries her words across. He has a little boat made of pine
and painted blue. He sings and lifts the coin
off her tongue: "You know how to whistle don't you Steve?" Toads
padding on the riverbank. "You just put your lips together… and blow." She says. A red halo
slipped with smoke.

176. "Dear sirs," by whom Mr. G really means himself, "it seems I'd like to tell you a story. See! here he comes now, the hero I mean, and his monomaniac horse. They are something gone unaffected by time. Naturally we are wary. Mr. G finds himself in the bathroom mirror wading thick in an unequivocal beard and steely blade." It was time for a shave. He goes right up to the window and knocks on the door: "No one answers."

177. The problem with "Hamlet is not Hamlet" "but rather that thing running atop time." Its hollow-eyed gestures, dead and with a poisonous ear. Stand and unfold yourself! but there is nothing much to say. "The dust merely rolling out behind them.

178. You can hear the crack of each hair under the blade's steady gaze." "The horse twitches." He is dried out and punctured with cacti. Everything ends wrong the hero remarks as he settles into his hat. "Yes," this is where the story goes thinks Mr. G, his fresh blue robe caught loosely around his ankles.

179. The poor sad horse, he calls out anyway, "A storm of flies pursues." "How even in his most important scene—a heap of bodies on the stage after all—the ghost will not shut up with his O O O O O O O O," and young Hamnet feeling extremely cross and dead.

180. The hero coughs and his spurs twinkle. In a play within a play there is not a lot of room to escape. "The past will simply pound upon you until there is nothing left but a raw, flinty kernel where a cowboy dances a two inch waltz with his spine. Mr. G stares back at his face," cut to the finest measure.

181. "Nothing turns accordingly," he sighs and walks away, leaving the blade on the edge of the sink. "Many a fallen divinity couch beside his ankles." "Let them do with it what they will."

y

x

where x = epiphany and y = temporal correspondence

where x = I'm sorry to say and y = this is where our story really begins

What absolute

    n
    o
    n
    s
    e
    n
    s
    e

y

        nothing

        is ever right in the end

and well you

               know it.

        x

where x = James and y = and the Giant Peach

Mrs. G: Packed into a Ball of Her Own Happiness

Sits on the couch and nothingness.

    Pulls out her teeth.
    Twists them back in.

These are the facts. Mrs. G and the T.V. (everyday and the couch). "Nothing's on," she complains.
Or as Hawthorne once told her:

    "Happiness has no succession of events because it is a part of eternity."

"Dear Herakleitos," she wrote back, "the days echo with light. The grove outside the window
covered in tightfisted blackbirds. The ants all over the house. Their bent touch tiny, bristling,
running out of their bodies

    red black beneath my fingertips yes,

you were right—souls smell in Hades and the flashing blue light

of the blackbird's soft inner wing

The Chorus: Homer and a Field of Poppies Twisting, Nude
(It Was an Arch Bridge—Very Sophisticated)

For Mrs. G

Memory is a fat ball . of golden

flesh . that runs up and down . our bodies . Watch

as she bends her steps . against the sky . She is lonely and . en route and

like most things . misnamed . Once she spent . 18 days building

a bridge . He tried to warn her (Proust):

"It was victory before it was a bridge, princess,"

but by then she had bought . all that steel . Watch . her leave and wave

goodbye for it is only . polite for memory . is memory . but

to be accurate . about such things she would be called . distance

crisp sky . in the sunlight

watch . but then . so would most .

O So Wonderfully Tired Was He

Mr. G makes the bell out of a giant pit of mud. It rings

into the ground. It is some sort of national holiday.

The boy helps thin the mud and smack it onto the bell.

"We're dying by inches!" they sing, laugh, take a coffee break.

The daughter sets the table. It is some sort of national holiday.

Mrs. G brings back a pie from the diner. The boy's mother

has just died. He sings in tiny inches to his train

under the pine tree. Count their childhood on your fingers and toes:

The lone waitress smoking with a fresh-faced pie for sale. James

holds out his hand. Her body feels cool and lean

under the pine tree. Their childhood falls down their necks

and into each other. It is winter and the wind hollows out the bell—

cold and leaning the sounds fold into her hands.

She is home. She is home. Mr. and Mrs. G call out

and into each other. It is winter and the wind holds

the daughter in its fist. James watches from the window

and bells come home come home. Mr. and Mrs. G

sweep themselves clean. The kitchen steams with food.

The daughter takes the day by her fist. She watches from the window

as it falls into the muddy pit of the bell. It's echo

sweeps them all clean. The kitchen steams.

Mrs. G changes out of her day clothes. Her apron

echoes into the muddy pit of the bell.

The peas are brightly green. Splattered over with freckles

the boy sits on top of Mr. G's apron. The day changes out

into night. They clink their glasses toward each other.

The peas are brightly green. The bird's skin is freckled and crisp.

There is nothing much to say. Mrs. G is sad but she is not surprised.

The night clinks the stars toward one another. The daughter

helps James build a castle out of her mashed potatoes. "Now the dragon dies"

she says. Mr. G is sad. There is nothing else to say.

He misses the boy. He misses his daughter.

The castle turns into a dragon. Its sunken belly built with mud.

Ring. Ring. Ring.

The boy misses Mr. G. The daughter misses

the sea with its open face and wide halls.

Ring. Rang. Rung.

Who's there?

The sea. An open face runs the house wide. The sea who?

Mrs. G drops the phone into her lap. She's been dead

for a long time. Who's there?

The day takes them gently back. As it always does.

Mr. G drops his head into her lap. The dirt

runs up his skin. The daughter comes home

as she always does. The house takes her gently back

to the boy. He smacks her heart into a bell:

come home. The sound runs up Mr. G's face

and into a giant pit of mud. It rings

Long Live the Weeds and the Wilderness Yet

At a certain point they both start forgetting things. Mr. G forgets his toes are beautiful. Mrs. G forgets she is not lonely. Occasionally they see a play and pretend to be grateful for the distraction. They go on long walks together. What's the name of the village down there? I don't know but there seems to be a garden. They eat hamburgers and french fries in silence. Mr. G can go an entire meal without telling her there's mustard on her chin. This is what we call living in the present. Taking each moment and rubbing it into our cheeks until our face turns a red violence. Mrs. G stands on the porch. There are some birds, some tall grass. She is quite yellow and expected. He is plopping through their potato field. Dropping each round body and shoveling it under with dirt. Mrs. G turns inside to make a sandwich. The day leaves as usual.

The daughter: The Hardship of Solitude

The collector sleeps inside
the hull. He visits
me by day. Carpet
spiking thinly into stomach

and elbows. Sunlight. Charts.
"And I can see
my soul is green
like Bulgaria." "One should

always distrust people who
know things," the collector
quotes and nods his
head into the sky

angels bouncing wisely. "Inevitably
they are cruel." So
it goes everyday as
we climb the masthead

together, hair moldy from
trapped seawater. "It feels
so special," I'd say,
"living inside an open

tomb. Now it's your
turn." And the collector
would undress swift and
sad being born of

the sea. His violet
skin shaking through the
twilight. Foam at his
neck. Air,
            like bells.

The Collector: It

"read: again, on top of," Anne Carson, *Economy of the Unlost*: "So the verbs for 'to read' in Greek typically begin with a prefix… [meaning] 'again' or 'on top of' as if reading were essentially regarded as a sort of sympathetic vibration between letters composed by a writer and the voice in which a reader pulls them out of silence" (83-4). Carson continues in a footnote to this remark: "It is fashionable to interpret this relationship between written text and reader's voice as a 'question of power' wherein the reader is dispossessed of his own voice in order to facilitate realization of the inscription…. The remarkable humorlessness of this line of interpretation seems to belie… the spirit of freedom in which artists… play through the possibilities of meaning available conjointly to writer and reader within a piece of language"

"rib of rock" is from Keats's *Hyperion: Book II*: see "Forest Hung Upon His Head"

"…rolling into parcels of pure sky" from Edmund Spenser's "An Hymne in Honour of Beautie":

> But when the vitall spirits doe expyre,
> Unto her native planet shall retyre;
> For it is heavenly borne, and can not die,
> Being a parcell of the purest skie (ln 102-5)

"rusty treasure": in Beowulf's last adventure he fights a treasure-hoarding dragon. While Beowulf kills the dragon, he too dies of a wound inflicted in the battle. The treasure, originally owned by an ancient and now extinct race, turns out to be rusty and corroded. This is Beowulf's legacy to his people

"saving shawl of the sea-nymph Ino" comes from Allen Mandelbaum's verse translation of *The Odyssey*. This line is listed as one of the summarized plots in Book V

"she had only to want something—in the beginning it mattered not what" is a slanted version of a quote by Nietzsche found in Judith Butler's *The Psychic Life of Power*. This idea revolves around the catch-22 of subject-making. In order to knowingly exist—to be able to say "hello, and my name is"—"one" must first want something outside of one's (not-yet-formed) self. The particulars of this desire do not matter; what matters is the desire itself: the realization of the hand grasping: "hey, I want that." Thus we become fully formed. The catch: we contain something not of ourselves—some foreign entity from which (because it is foreign) we always will remain alienated

The Chorus: I've Done Nothing but Contradict Reality from the Outset

People think the imagination is imaginative. For example, the
newfangled man took his nose into the air. People and their slender feet
tucked between their thighs laid with dew. People

are wrong. For example, the imagination is the detritus
of a reality firmly settled to a place. For example,
the lamplight made fish scales of the wall. This cannot be

overemphasized. For example, the disappointment came
from the white feathered mouse-tail of his touch. Here is the thin-laced gesture
of our quiet fate: night

so long our roome did fill. Likewise, at the time
of my birth there were eggs, mountains, crabgrass, titanic steel, microwaves, sensibility, points.
Everything clamored together, or what Milton

condescendingly calls, "the jingling sound of like endings"—making a mirror
where there is none: the houses merely throwing themselves open like a kind of wild
violet—"See! how the light falls out of us now!" Outside, my eyes plop

through a mottled field. Outside, there is no threshold from which
to exit: I take your hand—this is what is meant by: looking away. I take
your hand: the cave moves steadily on with a ripening winter.

Strophe: Much Turning of the Head from Side to Side

The problem with journeys is that sometimes you never come back. Therefore it is not so much a journey, as a long line of forever. One event touches another with no particular accumulation, no returning gesture: a cypress folds into the ground; a butterscotch lollipop smacks the air. This list is called the future, a truth many of us learn to maneuver around. For instance. Here is your prospect slightly bent and in your pocket. Now that it is yours, you must rename it. Option 1: "The sailors at the masthead ask, pointing their glasses to the horizon: Is there land or is there none? to which, if we are prophets, we make answer 'Yes'; if we are truthful we say 'No.'" or Option 2: "The road is before us! / It is safe—I have tried it—my own feet have tried it well—be not detain'd!" The answer, true with all except absolutes, is it depends.

You will pick the latter if, like Whitman, you live in the present tense. In all probability, you will be a good person. You can meet a sorrow in the eye and walk with it. You are Leopold Bloom: meaning you don't exist. Pretending not to be himself in an anonymous editorial: "Have you heard of this marvelous new author, Walt Whitman?" All the while his large naked body strutting behind his shirt. And so the present, well intentioned as it may be, always disappears.

Yet: "Mr. Joyce, I can understand why the counterpart of your Stephen Dedalus should be a Jew,

but why is he the son of a Hungarian?" "Because he was." Italo Svevo, who also didn't exist, but

Ettore Schmitz, his real name, did. He who wore the moustache Joyce gave to Bloom.

Or, perhaps the former—and you are Virginia Woolf. You look toward the future and

see the past; the present is not even a minor concern. In other words: Faulkner's Miss

Coldfield, who we always will find sitting the summer away in the house's hottest room with the

windows closed and the blinds closed because this is what the past demands. "The only romance

that George Eliot allowed herself," said Woolf. Imagine living your entire life with that fog at your

face. A body heavy with dust. Is it any wonder you are not a good person? Are you surprised to

learn you drag your brother down to the bottom of River Floss? For it is unlikely that it was Tom

Tulliver who would not let go.

Now all the good people are horrified. The best of you are even sad—here, take my strawberry handkerchief—it is a symbol of my love for you. The problem with journeys is that sometimes you do come back, but your destination is gone. Good people!, at the very least hope she remembers to look up at the sunlight slipping into the river. "To burn always with this hard, gem-like flame, to maintain this ecstasy, is a success in life." She says to her stone skirt, "like marbled eyes."

The daughter:

1. Virginia Woolf

2. Lycidas

3. Maggie Tulliver

4. Paul Celan

5. Ahab

6. Percy Bysshe Shelley

7. Ophelia

8. All of Odysseus' men

9. Egyptian Army (and Pharaoh?)

10. Everything, except Noah et al.

The Collector: Deep

"so, over that art / Which you say adds to nature, is an art / That nature makes" William Shakespeare, *The Winter's Tale*. Spoken by Polixenes to Perdita regarding the young girl's gardening habits. Polixenes' speech reflects the then popular idea that art, in this case gardening, improves nature and in doing so acts as an agent of nature

"strained by his beauty" is from Gerard Manley Hopkins' "The Loss of the Eurydice":

> … one sea-corpse cold
> He was all of lovely manly mould,
> Every inch a tar,
> Of the best we boast our sailors are.
>
> Look, foot to forelock, how all things suit! he
> Is strung by duty, is strained to beauty,
> And brown-as-dawning-skinned
> With brine and shine and whirling wind (ln 73-80)

"suppose in silks or tissues and costly embroideries" is from *The Arte of English Poesie* by George Puttenham (1589). In setting up his argument for artificially improving nature, Puttenham presents women's dress as an example of how humans enrich the naked state of nature

"swift and sad being born of the sea" refers to Algernon Charles Swinburne's "The Triumph of Time": "The loves and hours of the life of a man, / They are swift and sad…" (ln 73-4)

"there Is Something in God That Is Not God" is F. W. J. von Schelling via Slavoj Žižek ("The Abyss of Freedom"). See "She had only to want something." Similar to Hegel's idea of subject development, but predating it, Schelling questions how the Absolute (God) changes from nothing into a something, or, in other words, how God goes from "God" to "God Existing." Like Hegel, he comes to the conclusion that in order for the Absolute to consciously exist something foreign had to enter into the equation. So the play would read:

> (Act I)   Nothing.
> (Act II)   Nothing somehow (why, why, why) wants Something
> (Act III) Nothing's desire causes a reaching out and taking of Something
> (Act IV) Obtained, this foreign Something makes Nothing foreign. So the catch-22 of getting to be God Existing is that God is also Not-God
> (Act V)   Everyone dies but Prince Fortinbras

To a Sub-Sub Librarian:

It will be seen that this mere painstaking burrower and grub-worm of a poor devil of a Sub-Sub appears to have gone through the long Vaticans and street-stalls of the earth, picking up whatever random allusions he could anyways find in any book whatsoever, sacred or profane:

So fare thee well, poor devil of a Sub-Sub, whose commentator I am.

Thou belongest to that hopeless, sallow tribe which no wine of this world will ever warm; but with whom one sometimes loves to sit, and feel poor-devilish, too; and grow convivial upon tears; and say to them bluntly, with full eyes and empty glasses, and in not altogether unpleasant sadness—

Give it up, Sub-Subs!

Not to be outdone by anyone, the daughter finds and kills the Cyclops. She breaks Calypso's heart. The saving shawl of the sea-nymph Ino. Nightfall. Her parents send her newspaper clippings. They talk on the phone once or twice a week. What are you having for dinner? Eventually she will build everything into a play. It will climax in a small town in Kansas, where a loyal swineherd will serve her tea. Tennyson, too, will have a role. As will Homer and Joyce. Each one plays a Siren whose job is to fling their soft, round breasts to the ground like a red velvet curtain. "How dull it is to pause, to make an end," they say as she lashes their bodies with the stage floor. "The moral" says the daughter "is the end is always a lie."

"this is the general sense but not the exact order of…" "…the songs he sang" from the Venerable Bede's *An Ecclesiastical History of the English People* (complied 731 CE). Bede presents the songs of Caedmon—an illiterate cowherd who wakes up from a dream to find he is a gifted singer. The aforementioned quote immediately follows the song's appearance

"this was a very stupid story he didn't care to hear it again" George Eliot, *The Mill on the Floss*. The he is Tom Tulliver who, unlike his sister Maggie, has a limited love of learning: "[…] wonderful fighting stories about Hal of the Wynd, for example, and other heroes who were especial favorites with Tom, because they laid about them with heavy strokes. He had small opinion of Saladin, whose scimitar could cut a cushion in two in an instant: who wanted to cut cushions? That was a stupid story, and he didn't care to hear it again. But when Robert Bruce, on the black pony, rose in his stirrups, and, lifting his good battle-axe, cracked at once the helmet and the skull of the too-hasty knight at Bannockburn, then Tom felt all the exaltation of sympathy"

"to a Sub-Sub Librarian" refers to Herman Melville's *Moby Dick*. Prior to the story's opening, a brief preface appears followed by a series of extracts—all on whales/leviathans. The preface claims, with hyperbolic and enthusiastic hostility, that "a poor devil of a Sub-Sub" (librarian) gathered these extracts. This playful aggression is made all the more ridiculous and devastating when we consider this "mere painstaking burrower and grub-worm" is Melville, another kind of Ahab who is foolish enough to chase such a huge beast of extracts and fragmented knowledge. See Ahab

Virginia Woolf, author, 1882-1941. Fills her pockets with stones and drowns herself in the nearby River Ouse

"what Exile from Himself Can Flee?" Lord Byron, *Childe Harold's Pilgrimage*, Canto I (ln 857)

"what to do with an analyzed soul" is taken from William Wordsworth's *The Two-Part Prelude* (1799). The exact phrase: "Hard task to analyse a soul" (ln 262)

"…which be the flowers, as it were, and colors that a poet setteth upon his language by art" is from *The Arte of English Poesie* by George Puttenham (1589). Again, Puttenham, following the Elizabethan trend, is arguing how art and artificiality enhance nature

ACKNOWLEDGEMENTS

Grateful acknowledgment is made to the following journals in which these poems first appeared: *Drunken Boat*: Long Live the Weeds and Wilderness Yet; The Daughter: After Three Hours She Curtsied Profoundly and Left; Mr. G: The Bottomless Gulf of His Paunch. *Past Simple*: Mrs. G: In Greek Mythology. *Now Culture*: The daughter : the reader. *Sawbuck*: Hallelu, Hallelu, Hallelujah: The Chorus Sings for Mr G in Signs of Six; *Strophe*: Much Turning of the Head from Side to Side. *Shampoo*: Mrs. G: Then, Option B or the Loss of a Loss; The Daughter Begins/Ends Her Journey from All Three Sides; The Daughter: the Hardship of Solitude; The Chorus Plays Its Part. Six Finch: A Story As Wide As Air. *Slope*: Mrs. G: Packed into a Ball of Her Own Happiness. *Thermos*: Mrs. G as Young Glynis Young; How to Persuade an Abstraction. *Word for/Word*: We Must Look into the Matter: Reading Mrs. G Through the English Canon; The Chorus: Homer and a Field of Poppies Twisting, Nude; A Forest Hung Upon His Head.

ABOUT THE AUTHOR

Becca Jensen's poems have been published in *Thermos, Slope, Horse Less Review* and *Sixth Finch* among others. She lives in Nashville with her husband.

Post Office Box 7736
Los Angeles, CA 90007
www.lesfigues.com